SPIRITUAL LETTERS OF HOPE AND HEALING

I'm thinking of you

HERBERT BROKERING

Augsburg

MINNEAPOLIS

Dedicated to Harley Racer, my doctor for thirty-five years:

who helps me find enzymes in thankfulness and laughter,
who remembers stories of my family and knows all by name,
who speaks of my parents whom he never met,
who embraces me when I leave,
who talks about books and theatre while listening to my heart,
who praises progress and change in my spirit,
who teaches me exercises of health that live in me,
whose eyes shine with expectation when we see each other,
who thirty years ago helped me draw pictures of healing I could see,
and who knows these letters are true.

I'M THINKING OF YOU
Spiritual Letters of Hope and Healing

Scripture quotations are from the New Revised Standard Version Bible, copyright © 1989 by the Division of Christian Education of the National Council of the Churches of Christ in the U.S.A. and used by permission.

Cover and interior design by David Meyer

Library of Congress Cataloging-in-Publication Data
Brokering, Herbert F.
    I'm thinking of you : spiritual letters of hope and healing /
Herbert Brokering.
        p. cm.
    ISBN 0-8066-1999-6
    1. Sick—Prayer-books and devotions—English. 2. Brokering, Herbert F.—
Correspondence. 3. Consolation. 4. Health—Religious aspects—Christianity. I. Title.
BV4910.B755   1996
242'.66—dc20
                                                                                                96-5135
                                                                                                    CIP

The paper used in this publication meets the minimum requirements of American National Standard for Information Sciences—Permanence of Paper for Printed Library Materials, ANSI Z329.48-1984.   ∞

Manufactured in the U.S.A.   AF 9-1999

00   99   98   97   96   1   2   3   4   5   6   7   8   9   10

Contents

These letters are for you. Each letter explores a step—an experience—on your journey back to health. The list below can help you choose the most appropriate readings for your various moods and experiences. Or you can simply leaf through the book, reading from beginning to end. Either way, you will find words of comfort, insight, assurance and hope—reminders that you are not alone on this journey.

A Word from the Author

These letters began long before they were written down.

In 1983, I returned from a trip to Japan and China with a serious heart problem. During the long thirteen-hour flight back to San Francisco, our group travel escort was a guardian angel who never left my side. I felt that God was on watch through Barbara. I wondered: Who gave this woman such a compassionate spirit? Who are this woman's parents? That flight was the beginning of this book. Twelve years later, I wrote the letters to Barbara's mother, Bonnie.

When we reached San Francisco, I was taken to a hospital for a week of tests. On a visit to my bedside, the hospital chaplain put his finger to my forehead and said, "Herb, be there (he pressed gently) when you take the treadmill test." He urged me to be aware—to be centered—through the ordeal to come. I can still feel the pressure of his finger on my forehead—on the spot where I had been baptized. His touch reminded me of God's presence. It was what I needed: I was "centered."

After the tests, I returned home for heart surgery. Friends and family were like a sacrament of grace before and after surgery. My family doctor told me about the power of enzymes and joy and laughter, he drew pictures of healing, and he called my attention to each step in my recovery. He kept the guardian angel alive in me. My family kept pressing a finger to my forehead, reminding me that much of my healing was there—in the power God gave me to think and feel wholeness.

Three years ago I underwent an operation for prostate cancer. When I first heard the word "cancer," I went deep into my mind (that finger to my forehead), seeking the reservoir of God's healing power. I pictured health, beauty, music, love. Most of all, I pictured love: loving faces, persons, places, acts—and, above all else, a loving God.

A new world of relationships has opened for me. The flight from Japan, the finger on my forehead, the medicine inside joy and laughter, the healing power of touch and prayer—these things have taught me: God's angels are real, they are among us; they are like us.

Twelve years after the trip from Japan, our family was vacationing on the north shore of Lake Superior. I heard that Barbara's mother Bonnie had undergone the same kind of heart surgery I had, and she was not healing quickly. I'd met Bonnie only briefly when she'd visited Minneapolis from her home in Louisiana. I remembered again that flight to San Francisco and the person, who had stayed by me every second of the way. I remembered wondering: "Who are her parents? Who gave her such a spirit?"

The October leaves along the shore of Lake Superior were in full color. The air was brisk, gulls screaming and playing in strong gusts. All around and inside me was such power, force, love. I wanted to share it. And I wanted to pass on to Bonnie what her daughter had done for me. I made a sudden commitment to write twelve letters to Bonnie, to send one each day.

I began writing that day.

As I wrote, images of healing came to me from childhood. The love and joy of being in a creative family fed my writing. Each letter was a healing for me. Each writing was devotional.

Twelve days passed. Then weeks and months went by, and I continued to write. Some letters I sent, others I kept. Always I wrote as though to her—and to readers such as you. In all, I wrote 150 letters. Sixty of those were selected for this book. Those letters, which once began "Dear Bonnie," are now titled "I'm thinking of you."

And they are meant for *you*. They are written to you as well as to Bonnie. It is true, that as I travel the world in pilgrimages—as I so often do—I'm thinking of you. And as I reflect and write in this Minnesota valley—this home of thirty-five years, where we raised four children—I'm thinking of you.

The words "I'm thinking of you" are also the promise of the one giving you this book—someone close to you, someone who loves you. Most of all, they are God's promise to you—an echo of the beautiful promise in the final verse of Matthew's Gospel: "Remember, I am with you always, to the end of the age."

So as you read these spiritual letters of hope and healing, press a finger to your forehead and remember the promise: I'm thinking of you.

Herb Brokering

I want you to be well

This is my first letter to you. There will be more. I have a good reason for writing you: I want you to be well. Getting well is a personal adventure, so I am staying close to you in the letters to come. The first letter is my commitment to stay by you, because I want to, in your sickness and in your healing. I have agreed with myself, made a deal, to write you regularly. As you heal, I will give you my best thoughts and receive yours in turn.

Your mind and mine together will help in the healing. Others will give you their best thoughts and wishes. I want to be sure you have mine.

I picture you glad for this letter and feeling good that I am writing you. I imagine you improving in some way even as I write, even as you begin reading this letter. I believe in my heart that through these letters we will give peace to each other.

I am reaching to touch you, hear you, be with you. Do you feel me with you? Be open to the healing of touch, as today somebody talks to you and hears you. Let them be near you, as

I am near you in this letter. Receive their hug, touch, comfort, kind word, smile. Be receptive while others come, fragile and with special gifts for you. Feel persons reaching to you. Receive them as you would receive me. Healing is an exchange, a bridge, a circle.

This letter comes from inside my heart to your heart. I feel good writing you. I feel inside out. My wish is that this letter will reach into your mind and spirit. I want to be part of your healing circle. I am part of your miracle. That is my wish and commitment.

It is raining lightly. The lettuce is marking a spring green line in the garden. Sun and the rain have opened the seed. Lettuce is such a nice shade of green. Keep your mind on what is alive and growing.

I'm thinking of you.

It's good to be home

It's good to be back home, with plants and flowers you know. We leave; we return. The African violet waits. Plants wait until we return; they wait to please. Some wait for our return to bloom. It's good you are home to see the flowers.

Wrens are nesting near me. The first nest this spring. How they sing as they work. Can you hear them? They sing when finding sticks, when hunting food. Their life is a concert. They sing, sing, sing. Wrens sing to live through their seasons.

Today I'm sending you verbs: Sing. Bloom.

Sing: that's what wrens do to live. Bloom: that's what flowers do to live. Living is a natural thing for birds and flowers. To bloom—to open up the beauty inside myself—is not always an easy thing for me. Flowers just do it. Wrens just sing.

We decide whether to live or not. Nature just lives. We decide whether to open or not; plants just flower. We decide whether to express ourselves or not; birds just tweet. To express the words and emotions inside myself is not always to make a joyful noise, but the possibility is there no matter what sound comes out.

We have a double wonder: sometimes to be locked in, sometimes to be free. That's a possibility that birds and flowers don't have; they are closed into a fixed pattern. We don't repeat the same, set meter in life that wrens and roses do.

Illness makes a difference inside us. Some patterns change. We can grow with the new patterns and hold onto the old ones. I write hoping you will hear a bird today, or see a blossom open.

Birds need to sing.

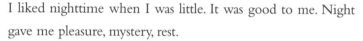

The beauty of night

I liked nighttime when I was little. It was good to me. Night gave me pleasure, mystery, rest.

How are your nights? How is the dark to you? I believe that night is meant to be our daily friend. I want you to believe this, too.

Remember playing games until it grew dark—and, if possible, well into the night? Do you recall the sunsets we saw then, the sheer beauty of colored horizons, the pinks and blues swallowed finally by a quiet, gentle dark? Can you still see the night turning deep purple as distant lights appear one by one—sparkling, dancing, shooting stars? We liked the night when we were young.

Night has its beauty, its quietness, even now. Night has meaning for our intellect, emotions, and spirit. Night is regal, mysterious, awesome. Night puts us near ourselves and close to those who love us. Close to God. Night is a Sabbath, a resting time. Night is sacred. Night is meant to be a dear friend.

Remember when we were little how it felt to be inside the house with our family at night? Night is safe. I wish for you the feeling of safety in the night.

In another letter I'll write about how we may use the night while lying awake.

The oak tree outside my window makes strong shadows when the moon is bright. I see it best in the winter when its leaves have fallen. Then it's clear to me how strong the oak stands, how strongly its magnificent branches reach out. Now, with the new leaves, its shadows and its branches are strong—but also soft.

Have a good night.

Healing pictures

Thank you for writing. Yes, I understand how quickly the fear and worry can set in. I wish for you the medicine of imaging, of seeing, of visualizing, beauty. Inner and outer sights of beauty heal.

After my heart surgery twelve years ago, I walked our Minnesota valley in my mind, looking toward recovery, seeking images of healing. At first I pictured geese in September rising in flight. I heard their loud journey songs ascending, their wings whipping like sails against the wind. The sounds and images were too strong for me. I was still too fragile. My emotions and mind could not keep up with their powerful flight.

So I chose a more quiet image. I pictured the presence of someone I admired: the whole person, close up. I walked in the valley concentrating on that person's face and that person's feeling toward me. My breathing became smoother, deeper, more natural. Finally I had found a healing image. I allowed the picture to be inside me and to comfort me.

While I walked I also pictured that person speaking words of reassurance and promise: "You can do it." I spoke the words aloud —"You can do it!"—in the person's sure tone of voice. The sound of those words was calming. I became more well.

There is a healing picture to carry you through the shadows of the valley in which you walk. The image of a friend before you, maybe inside you, can be a blessing from afar. Healing images often best appear in silence and behind closed eyes. Try it. Trust that a right image will come to you. Expect it. Wait. Your picture will arrive.

I encourage you to look forward to growing well. In your letter you showed concern for the African violet. I have found a window it likes, where it can see the sun. The violet has four white blossoms.

Picture your healing.

More healing pictures

We've talked about images that unlock a medication in the mind. The whole body benefits from a good imagination. How quickly a positive picture heals, or a right word makes us better. In my last letter, I wrote about an image that helped me recover from my own surgery. I want to say more things about healing images.

I was giving a Bible devotion. I spoke a phrase from Psalm 23—"my cup runneth over"—and asked people in the room to describe what that phrase made them see. A woman said, "'My cup runneth over' makes me see a huge bowl of patience. That's what I see: patience. So much patience that it's running over the edge of the bowl." A woman near her reached into her friend's space and said: "May I dip my fingers into the bowl? I need patience." With that, she reached into her friend's imaginary bowl and dipped out a handful of patience. Even the look of tension on her face seemed to soften and heal. Both women were sure the phrase they imaged had made them more well.

When I was in the hospital for spine surgery, I had a room-mate who talked about healing images. We shared what we saw in the words "The Lord is my shepherd." He saw the captain of his naval destroyer standing with him on deck during battle. They knew each other by name. His captain was wise and car-ing, a good shepherd. He said the captain saved his life—the lives of all the crew. That was his healing image for the shep-herd. Mine was different. "The Lord is my shepherd" brought to my mind an image of our night nurse. The nurse who spoke my name in the dark and told me how I was doing. I could read through all the verses of Psalm 23 and see her.

Why do so many people love the words of Psalm 23 when they are healing? The Bible is a healing picture book.

These words help make me well: Shepherd, Yes!, Roses, Waterfall, Quilt, Clover, Thanks!

Thanks to you.

The chance of a lifetime

Sometimes I hide pain with small talk. I make a joke to cover grief. I act brave to keep others at arm's length. I change the subject to prevent tears. And all of this is foolish. It offers no relief.

When we are most sick, it is time to make the most sense. It is time to be honest. Isn't this a chance of a lifetime? We may not have this kind of opportunity again. Illness is an important time in our life.

What do you think about in your pain?

Illness is a time to say what we believe, a time to talk about what matters most—to speak of values, principles, personal creeds. Sickness is a time to test, value, affirm, release, believe.

Illness is a time to relate to people and to God, a time to be open, to choose, to act, to decide.

All this leads to the question of most importance to me. When I am sick, the question I ask is "Who am I?" This is the time to picture and to speak of hope, health, life, love, spirit, salvation, future. These are healing images. And each is part of who I am. When I am sick there is time and there is reason to reflect on these parts of me—to see how each looks, how each fits with the others, how each makes up part of me.

What you say and hear is important, especially now. This time may be you at your best.

I am wishing you openness.

A time to cry

Since we last spoke, I have decided: sometimes a person has to cry. Sometimes we have to admit out loud: "I'm afraid. I'm sad. I need to cry. Let me cry. Crying is part of my story."

How does it feel to you when well-meaning people say, "Don't cry" or "You're not really afraid" or "It's not so bad" or "Things could be worse"?

People tell me "Don't cry" when crying is the one thing in the world I really need to do. They say "You're not really afraid" just when I feel fear filling my whole body. Honest expressions of crying and of fear are openings to our true story. These openings help us—and others who care about us— explore and understand the story we are living.

How do you keep your own true story flowing? This is what works for me.

If I hear the words "Don't feel that way," I say: "But I do feel that way. I do. I do." If I hear "Don't cry," I insist: "But I feel like crying. I need to cry. I am crying. Let me cry."

If your honest tears are interrupted by the words "Don't cry," then cry more, cry more. There is a time to cry. When it is my time, I offer no explanations, no apologies. There are rooms where people go to scream and shout. There are also crying rooms for people of all ages. The body is one such room.

And then, there is also a time to stop crying. A time when you have cried yourself out. A time not to cry. Your heart and mind will know that time.

The Bible tells us that, upon hearing of his close friend's death, Jesus wept. Nobody told him to quit. Jesus cried, and he quit crying. He knew the time for each.

I wish that knowledge for you.

An exercise of peace

How is it that I am writing all these letters? How do strangers become friends?

We did not know each other well before these letters. We met in a summertime, for only brief minutes.

Later you had surgery and began recovery. I heard of a day when your spirit was down; I wanted to help raise it. I knew your body hurt; I wanted to take your pain. These letters have lifted my own spirit and lifted my own pain. I hope they have done the same for you.

I care about your spirit. When the spirit heals, the inside changes. Spirit is a word for breath, wind, life. Your spirit is healing. When the body heals, the outside changes. Body is a word for house, structure, form. Your house is healing.

In the old story from Genesis, Adam and Eve gave birth to sons: Abel and Cain. The name Abel means spirit, breath; Cain means house, form. These two children were meant to live together in harmony. The form, the outside, was to be at peace with the spirit, the inside. But things didn't work out that way. We know the story.

In your healing, the spirit and body are making peace. We were created to live rested, balanced, at peace. These letters are a peace-making effort. Writing you is half the letter. Your reading and believing is the other half. Together we are creating healing peace.

There's a strong wind outside. All the trees are bending. The willow is touching the earth in a dance. The life inside the limbs is in tune with the strong fibrous bark outside. The willow is weeping in the wind—an exercise of peace.

Peace to you.

Loving life

"I want to live." You said it to me on the phone. I heard you. You want to live.

I need to tell you from the heart how glad I am to hear you say, "I want to live." I'm glad you like your life. I'm glad you want to live. Our lives are greater than we see. We live in people whose names we have forgotten. We live in stories told about us, photos shared, and in the minds of children who were once our playmates.

I'm glad you want to live. I thank God that we were given life. We know special seasons, places no one else has seen, images that are our own, and thrills only we have felt. You have a whole life inside you, one which already has seen you through months and years, hard and good times. The life given us will not end. When we die, the life will not quit: that's a promise. How glad I am for your love of living.

I want to hear you talk about your life, your faith journeys, your favorite times, hard places, miracles, best friends, ancestors, true stories, struggles, favorite flowers, dreams. I want to feel your feelings about life, your wants, your loves. I want to hear more about your life—things you have not told me. Tell me more about your life.

"I want to live." We have a right to want life, expect life, cherish life. After all, God gave us this taste and zest for life. We are to live each day as if it were our whole life. Each day, each time of day, is our lifetime. God promises us we will live and live fully. I have this same promise as you have. Your desire to live makes the promise more sure for me.

Thank you for the wonderful words, "I want to live." I wish for all who live that they, like you, would truly *want* to live.

Life is for loving.

Surprised by beauty

Yesterday I saw something little and beautiful which I might ordinarily have missed: one flower along my path. I memorized the blossom.

On this walk I specifically watched for tiny surprises—things I might miss unless I intentionally looked for them. A world of tiny prizes opened to me. I wish you had been with me. In this letter we are on that path together.

It was a slow and wonderful walk. I began by saying "Herb, go and see! Find beauty. See something tiny and beautiful. Enjoy it. Memorize the sight. Tell someone." I left my camera at home so I'd be sure to really look for myself.

I looked. And I write you about a tiny bit of what I saw. One single blossom spoke to me with its whole heart: "Hello. Hello." I felt fully greeted; it did not hold back. I was charmed by a tiny white blossom. It was my bouquet for the day, yet only my first surprise of many.

As I walked, I bent over other tiny sights of beauty. Each was waiting magnificently to say, "Hello. Here I am for you."

Beauty is often very small in the midst of everything else, but it can loom wonderfully large if you stay near it for a while.

On my next walk I assigned myself the pleasure of finding four different signs of beauty. And, do you know, four was only the beginning. My familiar walk was becoming something altogether fresh and exciting. My whole day was made new.

I wish for you to do the same: to go and see. Today let a tiny sign of beauty greet you. Let nature surprise you, touch you. Show someone, or tell them what you saw. Discover a little bit of beauty and see how it colors your whole day.

Today these familiar words of God have become new to me: "This is the day the Lord has made; I will rejoice and be glad in it."

I hope the flowers I saw make you glad. The oak outside my window is fully green now.

"Here I am." Every living thing knows those words.

Listen up-close

Today I am writing about things that are very tender, very fragile: my heart, my spirit, my most delicate feelings. (I wonder why we refer to the heart when we talk about emotions and passion.)

Today I listened to friends very closely, carefully, from the heart. I heard what they were saying to me about their feelings. I did not try to stop them or turn their words into my own. I listened to their hearts, and I listened to my own.

I saw their hearts, their passions, their inner selves. What they showed me was tender, delicate, fragile, alive. For the first time I listened up-close; I looked clearly at what I heard.

What did I hear? I can tell you that it was very, very beautiful. It was all heart. This was a time when I truly felt their spirits. I am glad I did not fill this time with my own agenda, my own concerns.

Today I truly listened, and I discovered why I like these friends so much—and why they like me. I saw into their hearts.

Many people come to us bearing tender spirits. We are a gift to them when we listen and look and feel their passions. It's a gift to feel the passion of others. There is a tender side to all of us. It takes time and care to uncover that side.

Today I looked closely and carefully at a bed of tulips. The nearer I came, the more their beauty expanded. Do tulips have a set number of petals? Does a tulip make a sound? Sometimes I stay too far away.

A friend is always close.

LISTEN

UP-CLOSE

Be close

When have we ever been closer? When have we ever understood each other so clearly as now when we are healing?

Distance does not divide good friends. Nearness is inside the mind. That's where our closeness lives.

This is our time for closeness. We'll dwell on close times with special persons. Picture distant friends as if they were with you—beside you—talking, touching, listening, looking. Picture being close to someone you miss and want and need and love.

This is a time for close talk. Whisper close feelings you heard that special person say. Whisper the words with feeling. Form each word with your lips so you recall the emotions the words bring to you. Hear good answers from your friends, family, lover. Hear the sounds of closeness. Closeness is in the mind and in the heart.

This is a time for loving words. Say endearing words to those who visit you. Speak kind words to anyone helping you. Say prayers for people you love. Write loving words to someone. Phone persons you love and say dear words to them. Admit to feelings of closeness with loved ones so they know you, trust you, and stay close to you.

Stay close to God. Say words you know by heart from the Bible. Whisper or hum lines from hymns you like. Stay close to a sacred word that quiets you. Rest inside the Word.

Be close to yourself. Enjoy your dearest memories. Dwell on emotions that made you healthy and happy. See yourself as someone intimate, dear, loving, lovable. Be close to yourself.

Get close to those you trust: a teacher who made a difference, someone who helped you pray, a friend who made you feel like family. Be close to someone who taught you to be close to God.

Violets are blooming under the oak.

This is a time for closeness.

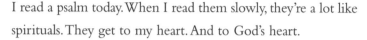

Where is God?

I read a psalm today. When I read them slowly, they're a lot like spirituals. They get to my heart. And to God's heart.

I hear reports that all is not well with you. Your spirit is down, progress seems too slow, and God too far off.

Are you asking, "Where is God? Why doesn't God do more for me?" When I hurt I want to know where God is, what God is feeling and doing about me.

We're all like that, I think. When we hurt, we want to know where God is. So what do I say? In this letter, only this: tell God you hurt. Tell God how you feel. Tell God if you are angry or afraid. Tell God what's on your mind, in your heart. Do it. Then we'll talk about this some more.

Is it all right to get angry with God? I have. I do. When I can't find the right words to speak my anger, I read the Bible. There are the psalms where singers kick against God; they cry out, whine, protest. Page through the psalms and hear the angry words you may be looking for.

After you kick and scream and say your piece, keep talking. Keep talking to God. Listen to what you say next. In the Bible you will notice that after the psalm writers protest and cry out against God, they keep talking. First they kick and scream; then they hug and love. They get to the hugging through the protests and cries.

Listen: Psalm 22 begins by asking God, "Why are you so far from helping me, from the words of my groaning?" But the song ends with, "All the ends of the earth shall remember and turn to the Lord; and all the families of the nations shall worship before him."

Where is God when you hurt? Tell God what it feels like to ask that question. Talk to God. Our words do not change the heart and mind of God toward us. But telling God may change our feelings and thoughts toward God. It's part of the cure.

I want to keep that question alive: "Where are you, God?"

Feeling at home

Dan phoned the other day from home. He reminded me of a time when their children were little: three girls. When I visited unexpectedly, the girls' shoes were scattered in the hallway. Dan was embarrassed. I said, "When their shoes are here, you know they're home." Dan remembered that one sentence from eighteen years ago.

You are home.

Even after all these days, it's hard to believe you're home. Home is a refuge. Find yourself a cozy nook, a window, a chair, a healing place. Be good to yourself. Make yourself at home.

Look around slowly. See how much you have to care for you: shelter, bed, food, friends, protection. Let something in your room become for you a sign of hope. See a flower as a bouquet. Read a greeting card as a visit. Be glad for fresh water, for a pillow. Choose a single sign in your room as a sacred symbol, a promise from God.

I may have told you this story about Julie. When she was critically ill and in traction, she focused on two cracks in the ceiling that were shaped like a cross. This became her spiritual symbol, her sacred sign. That sign empowered her, reminded her. She felt safe—at home.

Why not find a sacred sign inside your room today? I will do the same. We will feel our safety. We know the promise from Jesus: "I will be with you always." Let's find signs to remind us of that promise, to remind us that we are home. We need to feel the power and healing in the promise, too.

You know, when I'm with other oaks, I feel at home. They are so alike; they remind me of the oak outside my window—my oak.

Welcome home.

A healthy spirit

My oak has a dead branch. I will call the tree doctor, who knows oak trees, so I know what to do about it.

Many years ago, friends and I were playing on the Atlantic beach. Suddenly I felt a pain in my left leg. I thought someone had hit me with a ball. Thrombosis. The doctor told me to keep my leg elevated for two months. I cheated. I was to keep it wrapped and to exercise it regularly. I cheated. I didn't have time for all that. I decided I could heal it my own way. Forty years later I still wear elastic hose—the price of doing things my way.

Sometimes we do dumb things because we feel we're losing control. We choose to take control, even if it's in a negative way or brings negative results. That happens when we become desperate and panic.

Some physical things cannot be changed. There are times when it's best to go with the situation, accept it, embrace it. We have the power to prolong real healing and increase the hurt when we struggle against reality.

I know what I'm talking about. Changes came with my cancer surgery. I have side effects I did not expect, want, or plan for. Overnight I became incontinent. I could not change this or control it. I accepted and embraced incontinence. Now I am open to research, growth, healing possibilities.

There is, however, a place in which we have great control: in our spirit. There is the power for our spiritual growing. As physical tissues decline, spiritual energy can be renewed, hope and vision can increase.

Go for spirit health as well as for body health. When we lose some physical function, our spirit can help us make peace with that loss.

Despite its dead branch, the oak tree does a very slow dance in the wind. The willow is waltzing in the same wind.

When we see each other next, let's dance.

See yourself well

Ouch! You know that word.

Do you ever wish to see what pain looks like? Do you want to picture how the body heals? I do. I want pictures of what's going on.

I got a clear picture after my spine surgery. I knew I could stand the pain if I could see the problem. I believed I would heal sooner if I could see the area healing. So I asked Doctor Harley to draw me a picture. He did. Immediately I began to see what I could control and what I couldn't. I saw the pain.

I pored over his drawing like an architect. I saw connections, causes, effects, possibilities. I saw how my body was wired for health. I began running pictures of healing like a film, over and over before my eyes. The pictures came in color.

I saw the pain; I saw beyond the pain. I saw through the hurt into the healing. The sequences were important. The visual frames of pain came first, then the getting well.

Ask someone to help you see what hurts. Get a clear picture of the area that is healing. That is the main focus for your inner eye. Then run your own film of healing images. Let the film run inside you, like a private showing. Be more than the audience—be the director, the actor. Make the film your own so you understand it, feel it, enjoy it.

Believe the pictures of your getting well. When Jesus said "Be healed," people believed; they saw themselves well. With believing came healing.

By the way, I'm writing little one-liners like this: "If you ever feel snowed, lie down, enjoy the sky, and make an angel." What do you think?

The oak keeps growing; yet it looks much the same as it did thirty years ago.

Be healed.

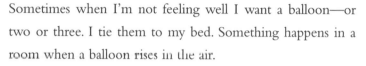

A bouquet of balloons

Sometimes when I'm not feeling well I want a balloon—or two or three. I tie them to my bed. Something happens in a room when a balloon rises in the air.

When I felt depressed and down during recovery, someone brought me a dozen red balloons, a balloon bouquet. The bouquet rose in the air above me. Nurses, doctors, and visitors looked up when entering my room, and they treated each other—and me—with a lighter spirit. We were all uplifted.

By evening there was only one red balloon left. I gave each visitor one balloon from the bouquet. That night, each of eleven homes had a red balloon. I had one, too.

It was a little like a Jewish Sabbath. The balloons were like candles at sunset, bringing light to homes all over town, making all the homes into one big family. As a red balloon rose in the air, I believe it lighted the spirit in each room.

Here's a red balloon for you. Take it to your room. Let it rise above you. Look up. Tap it in the air. Keep it overnight. Greet it in the morning. Then grant it freedom: give the balloon away.

I hope this balloon will lift your spirits and remind you of these words of Psalm 121: "I lift up my eyes to the hills—from where will my help come? My help comes from the Lord, who made heaven and earth."

Sometimes I'm up, sometimes I'm down. O yes, Lord.

Enjoy the balloon. Be lifted up.

A
BOUQUET
OF
BALLOONS

Embrace your pain

There is a brand new nest in the oak. The tree's leaves are dark green and full; they shield the new nest from sun and the east wind. The oriole is singing. This is its second nest. Monday a storm broke a branch of the oak and blew away its first nest. The oriole spent little time grieving. Now the air is full of bird music. You know the sound.

You mentioned that you sometimes hurt, and you feel a slight pain you'd thought gone. You said, "The pain came back, and I embraced it." That is what I heard you say. You faced your pain, said "Hi," and took it in. You did not try to keep it outside and fight it as an enemy. You took it into yourself to make the pain well. You can heal it when you accept it.

The Oriole sang as it built its new nest. It sang even though its home had been destroyed. It is still singing.

I had a pain that would not leave. It started with an injury, and muscles and nerves began a battle. The injury was healed;

the original cause of the pain was gone. But the battle of muscle and nerve kept on. I hurt. Then I spoke to my pain. I said, "Your reason is gone. The fight is over; the bell has rung." The muscles and nerves were embarrassed, it seemed. They quit the fight. My pain left.

That is how I imagined a healing scenario inside myself. And it helped me heal.

You said "Hi" to your pain. You told me how the pain felt. You named it and owned it as real. You took it in to make it well. I'm glad you believe in embracing real pain.

Breathe straight through your hurt, not around or over it. Breathe through it. Tell the pain you are there. And then tell it to heal. Your faith and God's power are greater than the pain.

The Oriole has a new home. It is singing in the oak.

There is a feeling stronger than pain.

Forget to remember

Thank God for the gift of forgetting.

You will not remember your suffering as much as your healing. So much of what you do not like, cannot bear, will disappear. Good will outlive the rest. Your positive thoughts will overwhelm the negative ones. You will remember feelings of healing and of laughter.

Perhaps this has happened to you, as it has to me. Someone I haven't seen for years greets me: "Herb, how's your back?" My back? Oh yes, that surgery twenty-four years ago. I'd forgotten. Someone else greets me: "How's your heart?" My heart? I haven't thought about my heart problems for months. That surgery was twelve years ago.

Look at everything that's happening now. Be open to more than the pain. Absorb what is good—the glances of kindness, touches of concern, gifts of love, the prayers of friends. Take them in. They will outlive your pain and tears.

Feel everything that is real around you and within you. Acknowledge all your feelings, your discomfort, loneliness, anger. Be open to what hurts so it will not hide inside you. Face the negative feelings, then let them pass through you. Do not fear them. They are not as strong as the healing and laughter and faith that are also inside.

The time will come when someone says, "How are you?" They'll be remembering the way you hurt. You'll remember the joy of healing. That's what happens.

Crows like perching in the oak. When they sing, their songs match the depth of the oak.

I am thinking positive thoughts about you.

I love you

Sometimes it's hard when family or friends leave a sick room to go home, or to go away for the weekend or longer. What are the best parting words for you when visiting hours are over? I think of what I saw and heard and said when people I loved left my sick room. This is what I remember.

I waved. I lifted my hand and held it in the air. I made the sign of the cross on someone. I stared. I looked away. I smiled. I held back tears. I said words like, "See you! So long! Come back soon! Thanks! Call me!"

I tried not to say "Good-bye." Good-bye is a word with noble roots—"God be with you"—but it doesn't always fit. It seems too final in a sick room.

Let me tell you the strongest parting words I heard from anyone when I was sick. These were always her parting words to me: "I love you! I love you!" I decided those were good parting words for me. Good words when you want to say the best there is to say.

"I love you!" That tiny sentence stays in the air, keeps sounding, grows in the mind, comes back through the night, lasts until morning, and gives life.

The words bring back memories. "Herbert, I love you!" That was the strongest sentence of my childhood. My name "Herbert" and the words "I love you" in the same sentence. Those words, the sounds, the feelings, have never left me.

"I love you!" That's how you've always signed off when we talk on the phone. Nice last words.

Today I planted a tree and named it Phileo, which means "friend." We will watch the tree grow.

I love you! I love you!

Ask questions

Our illness can make people we love feel helpless. They have to do things they're not used to. They're not used to waiting on us, sitting long hours alone, preparing their own meals, keeping things in order, maintaining a household. They want to do more than they're able to.

We all wonder about the feelings and behavior of our loved ones. Sometimes they flare up, are irritable, get bored, feel lost. I know. I've seen it happen, too.

Consider asking questions so you can hear their feelings and concerns. Those who are close to you may be worried, angry, disappointed, stressed. They may feel inadequate, helpless. They may even feel they somehow contributed to your illness.

We can ask and then listen. This is our special time to grow in understanding. Set simple rules for asking and guidelines for listening. I try questions that are not loaded, such as "How do you feel about my sickness? What is hardest for you? What do you most look forward to? How do you think you're doing? How can I best help you? What do you want to do now?"

One helpful question is all you need. Don't go for a big discussion or debate. Just be ready to listen. Keep the air between you open, loving, receptive.

How do we learn to ask well? I once asked an old tree six questions: "What's your name? How are you? Who visits you? When did you arrive? What was your hardest time? What's your best season?" With a little editing, all the questions were good for starting a conversation. Take time to find a good question—one that sounds and feels good. It's worth it.

There will be many leaves to rake from the oak this year. This once seemed a burden. Now I like it.

How can I best help you?

Health is all around

It's clear that God is big in your life. You talk about God being in all directions—past, present, and future. Yesterday you mentioned Sunday school songs, talks with a neighbor who's a minister, and a book about angels. You said, "God is all around me."

You make me think of the hours I spent in grade school marking circles with a compass and then making half circles and petals and flowers inside the big circle. How beautiful life was inside that big circle that reached to the edges of my tablet.

"God is all around." Your words inspired a prayer. You helped me write it. The prayer is about the great circle of God, a circumference, and it resembles an Irish prayer we both know.

God:

> Be the One before me to show me the way.
> Be the One beneath me to lift me up.
> Be the One for me to make me strong.
> Be the One with me to keep me standing.

Be the One behind me to bless my story.
Be the One above me to draw me higher.
Be the One within me to make me glad.
Be the One around me to make me whole.

The prayer uses eight prepositions under God. I liked prepositions in grade school. I like them now: they're about relationships—before, beneath, with, above, within. As children we played out our prepositions—"for, with, beside, before, around" our friends. Later we learned to spell and write prepositions, to use them in sentences, to diagram them.

Healing is about prepositions, about being in relationships.

All prepositions, taken together, shape a full circle. You said: "God is all around me." That's what the poem means.

Enjoy your life inside that great circle.

Loved ones are afraid, too

This letter is about Mavis and Gary. I know you care how my friends are doing.

In the morning, Mavis will be in surgery. I talked to her today, and she is not afraid. She knows that it may be serious, and she is facing it. Not just facing it, she's embracing it. Mavis has always been strong that way.

Her husband Gary won't talk about it. That's why she wanted to talk to me. Gary doesn't want her to talk about it with him—not openly, anyway. He won't say the word "cancer." Mavis needs to say the word "cancer" out loud. That sort of thing has always been their difference. He tends to hide unpleasantness; she embraces reality. I think I know why.

Tonight on the phone, Mavis told me that when Gary was a child, his mother was often ill. Illness didn't feel good to him then, and it doesn't now. Illness always frightens him, and he acts like it isn't real, isn't true. When Mavis talks about the surgery, he changes the subject. It's harder for him than it is for her. He's afraid.

Sometimes it's harder for the loved ones who are watching and waiting than for those who are going through the illness or surgery.

When nurses rolled me into by-pass surgery, I think I was singing. I don't think my family was singing. During the eight hours of my surgery, my family sat with friends who'd gone through the same surgery. The friends told them about their own miracle and brought sandwiches. The operation and the days that followed were harder on my family than on me.

Keep others in your prayers. Those who are visiting and caring for you are also in need of care and prayer. Even those who are physically healthy can hurt and worry and fear, and they want to be well also.

It's nine p.m. Gary will be back from the hospital soon, and I will phone and listen to him. Call me when you feel like it.

Sometimes I need your unexpected call.

LOVED ONES
ARE AFRAID,
TOO

Connected to others

You have never wanted to be a burden to others. You didn't want others to feel you couldn't make it on your own. You wanted to be self-sufficient.

Why do we feel we're a burden when others care for us? Why do we feel guilty when our lives make sudden demands on others? Why do we feel we have to make it by ourselves?

Life is a network, a fabric, an intricate connection.

Remember the lake we visited last summer? Remember how the lake was healthy, growing, clean, clear? Remember how we talked about everything in the lake as related, intersected, connected? We saw the lilies and water and tadpoles and turtles and logs and grasses and ducks all as one family. They belonged together. Together they all made up the lake.

So it is with you and me. We are like that lake—we are interconnected, related, together. We aren't isolated or separate. We can't live on our own. Remember how we loved the lake? I don't believe we thought any part of the lake felt inferior to the rest, isolated from the rest, guilty for needing the rest. When one element of the lake changes or shifts, the rest of the lake responds to accommodate it. Together, all the parts are in motion, making the lake constant and well.

We heal together. We get well when we're connected. In one of his biblical letters, St. Paul writes that when one member of Christ's body suffers, all parts feel it. Likewise, when one member heals, all get better.

We are like the lake that we loved. Do you remember the frog on the lily pad, and the log with the turtle sunbathing?

A groundhog lives deep under the roots of the oak. I often see it scamper off to a pond for a drink.

Remember the lake.

Signs that unite us

How many miles is it from me to you?

How can we be close when we're so far apart? Is there some way we can be together to draw strength from each other? Is there something we have within reach, something in common?

I'm asking you these questions because I know how much we can miss others, how much we can wish to be standing side by side with ones we love—especially during times like these.

What can we do to close the miles? There are common symbols that unite us. There are significant signs and times we share: things we can focus on together each day, times when we can agree to feel near each other. Here are some signs that can unite us:

> the sunrise
> the sunset
> two in the afternoon

when we see the first star
at seven in the evening
during our bedtime prayers
when we drink our morning coffee

These are just some possible times we can have together.
They can be daily markings that draw us close.

Together with your loved ones, choose times to be near.
Then practice nearness at those times. Feel each other's presence. Send good, healing thoughts; speak prayers together.
Listen for each other.

In this time of healing we can be nearer than ever.

There are six trees near enough to touch the oak. Or is the
oak touching the six trees?

I am close to you as you read this.

We aren't alone

Sometimes I want to be alone, really alone. I want to shut myself off, hide, separate, be all by myself. But it's impossible to be that alone.

You know what happens when I want to be all alone? Just when I want to disconnect completely, absolutely, someone thinks of me. Someone wants me or needs me. Someone repeats words I once said, does something I once did, remembers me. And just like that I am not alone.

It is impossible to be absolutely alone.

Once we get on the world, we can never get off. We can go somewhere to be physically alone, but we cannot disconnect ourselves completely.

Pieces of us are everywhere interacting with—together with—others in some way. Trees I climbed or planted are now giving shade to others, flowers I planted are now giving pleasure, words I wrote are now being read, songs I dreamed are now being sung, moods I expressed are now being shared, touches and hugs are now being remembered.

No, I cannot disconnect myself completely. None of us can. And we are fortunate that we can't.

There are embraces I received which still tingle, kisses I still smell, shared wine I taste, laughter I see, words written that I know by heart. I cannot escape the world I'm in and the community that I'm part of. When I want to be alone—really alone—I get reconnected.

Never believe that you are all alone. Now, in this moment, someone is thinking of you, feeling your presence, missing you, loving you.

Years ago you thanked me for a bottle of wine. I often think of your thanks. And I remember our phone conversation about heaven.

Call me sometime. Someone is thinking of you.

Send an invitation

If you want company, ask for it. I like it when you call me and say, "I miss you. Let's talk." Sometimes the patient needs to invite the friend. I'll never forget the invitation I got from a long-time friend who wrote, "Come and see me."

Joe was an old friend. When he became ill a few years ago, I'd visit occasionally. But when he got really sick, it was hard for me to visit. I'd never seen Joe like this. I didn't want to show my emotions and make him feel worse. I decided to wait until he was better before visiting again.

The more I stayed away, the more Joe was on my mind. I wondered how much he noticed my absence, cared, missed me. Then Joe wrote a note asking me to visit. An invitation. I visited immediately, and I told him my feelings. He told me how much he'd missed our talks, my presence, my voice. He said he needed my visits, and he made me believe he did.

I was comforted by his directness, openness, honesty. I needed to be with him, to see him in this new way. My visits made a big difference in both our lives. During his recovery we talked about things we'd never mentioned in the years we grew up together. I'm so glad he sent me that invitation.

Some of your friends and family may be behaving like I did. You wonder, "Why don't they come? Why don't I hear?" As with Joe and myself, perhaps they are staying away even though you both need each other. Do what Joe did. Ask them to come more often, or to write, or to phone. Admit your feelings. Say "I need you." It may be a big step ahead for both you and them.

Don't be afraid to send for someone you need. The Bible has lots of stories about sick people who sent for Jesus—and he came immediately.

The oak is silent today. There is no wind.

While the oak stood quiet, I whispered your name.

SEND AN
INVITATION

The need to help

Is it easier to give or to receive help from others?

I am sure that today someone needs to help you. They want to, and they need to.

When I want to help, you can help me by telling me how. Think about my wanting to help you. What do I have to give that you need? What can I say that you want to hear? What can I do that will please you?

Helping gets at deeper questions. Who am I to you? Who are we to each other? What is our relationship, and how can that relationship help you now? I want you to think about that. That's what is on my mind.

We are all in some kind of need. I need to give, to listen, to help, to heal you. I want to make you happy in some way. I want to because I'm connected to you; God made us both. And I'm your friend. We've been through thick and thin together. We know each other.

You helped many people with a word or action, even when you weren't aware of it. I began writing you because I felt your pain and wished for your healing. I thought—hoped—you needed me. That's why I am writing you now. I wish to care for you in some way that you want and need. I do.

Let me do something for you because I want to.

There is a tiny oak not far from the great oak. When autumn comes, I will move it to its own place. If I do that, it may outlive me.

Stay strong.

Families

Do you sometimes believe you're a burden to the family? Let's think about what "family" means.

Family is friends. When strangers become close, they become family. Family is people who give and take, show their best and worst. Family is what relatives have been to us and we to them. It's people who know each other completely, who need and want each other. In a real sense, family is a place where people don't owe each other: we don't keep records of credit and debit. Family is a place where we lean on each other.

Our family depends on us even when we are ill. Family members remember what we have been to them, have given them in the past, what we wish for and feel toward them, what we have done for them. However we are feeling today, whatever we are doing and being, we are contributing to our family. We are part of their history, their stories, their successes, their hopes. As they pray for us, their lives are strengthened. As they care for us, they improve. As they love us, their lives grow richer.

This is a time to receive, to thank, to be open, to lean, to require. Give yourself to your family. Give them who you are and what you can give at this time: your wants and needs, a smile, words of thanks, a touch. Give them what you have to offer today. That is all we can give each other.

Let your family care for you. It will make them well.

Today I wonder what I do for the oak in my family. This for sure: I love the oak in all seasons of the year. That's what I do for the oak.

I'm glad to be a part of your family.

Healing and being healed

When I was little I helped my mother when she had migraine headaches. I rubbed her neck with all my heart. I wanted to make her well. And as I helped make her well, I healed also. I still draw on that healing relationship these many years later. I can feel the touch. I can feel how she let me give her my healing.

That is what I want to write you: healing is relational. Healing goes both ways. When we accept help, we help the one who gives it. Healing is a cycle. It's a relationship of giving and accepting.

I did not force my efforts at healing on my mother. She did not resist when my small fingers were rubbing her aching neck. I gave; she received freely. All the while we healed, I heard the soft lyrics of her moaning: "Ahhmm. Ahhmm." She made the healing sound in sync with her breathing. I can hear the single sound now: Ahhmm. Ahhmm. Amen. That's what it sounded like when I was little. Amen. Amen. Amen. I still hear that healing sound.

I received the sound when I was little. Ahhmm—Amen is still a healing word, now that I am older.

Amen to you with all my heart.

Homemade cures

Do you remember the homemade cures of childhood? Some our family knew by heart. Others were kept in a worn medical book my mother knew as well as she knew the Sears Roebuck catalogue.

When we got the hiccups walking home from school, we knew a sure remedy to cure them: "Throw a clod of earth backwards over your right shoulder and hear it drop to the ground." And there was the footnote: "The chances of cure increase with the distance you throw the clod behind you." Those were the medical prescriptions of country kids.

We believed in the cures. So those with hiccups took turns being cured walking along the country road. Some thought the cure rested in the believing. Some thought it had to do with the clod of earth. Others discovered it had to do with holding your breath while you waited for the clod to land.

Whatever the truth, it was a remedy. And it had to do with believing, I am sure, or we would not have done it.

And it had to do with the clod of earth. Medicine needs a pill to swallow, an injection, a salve to rub— or a clod of earth to throw.

Healing had to do with breathing. The breath-holding broke the pattern of the hiccup.

Breathing is medicine. Sometimes it's a deep breath, sometimes a cough, a shout, a sob, a sigh. Sometimes the breath is laughter.

God is called Spirit.

Spirit, wind, breath—these are synonyms.

Hurrah for cures.

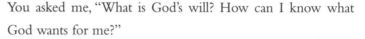

The will of God

You asked me, "What is God's will? How can I know what God wants for me?"

I also ask, "What is God's will?" There are a lot of ways to raise that question. When I pray, I try to get in touch with God's will—not just my own.

So what does one pray in an emergency, before surgery, when the healing isn't going well? I told you in another letter that I sang when I was going into heart surgery. Singing prayers. It's a good way to get in touch with God's will. Sing.

Another time my prayer going into surgery was more complicated. I pondered, prayed, tried to picture God's will. More than a song, my prayer was a complex image. I prayed, "Your will be done." Thoughts of God's will floated through my mind. Three streams of images came. In the first, I envisioned God's original will and ultimate plan for me and for all creation. I pictured images of perfection as God's will. The second picture series was of God's will working to heal the world today—a world full of fear, war, death, evil. I pictured the struggle as God worked to overcome evil and fear. In the third stream of images I saw God's ultimate will for me and for all creation: heaven, health, no more tears, light, life forever. I pictured the world perfected once more, and finalized through God's will.

Within seconds these images bathed my mind; I went to sleep imaging perfection. I felt "perfect," with both thumbs up!

The will of God is not a single sentence for me; the will of God is a host of images which I entitle "Perfect."

Thumbs up to you.

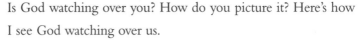

God is watching

Is God watching over you? How do you picture it? Here's how I see God watching over us.

Sometimes God watches like my mother or my father: quietly, with a warm drink and medicine, knowing exactly how I feel, pulling the quilt up to my chin and tucking it over both my shoulders. God is the one who never goes to sleep while I'm in need, and is always near enough to hear my every move.

Sometimes God is watching like my doctor: just down the hallway, on the way to see me, knowing the latest research, ready to call other doctors to help if needed, giving nurses exact instructions, sitting down beside my bed, looking right at me and giving me absolute attention, calling me by name, telling me how I'm healing, giving me hope, promising to return.

Sometimes God is like my good neighbor: bringing flowers or a special treat each visit, telling me stories about what's happening outside, promising to bring me a dinner when I'm home again, knowing just how long to stay, believing I'm looking better, telling me the truth in an upbeat way, waving one more time on the way out. How is God watching over you?

God has enough angels to take care of us all, and once in a while, we're fortunate enough to see them and know who sent them. God fills the air with good news, good sounds, and good will, which we can see and feel if we look and receive. God made us and provides all we need to live and die without being afraid. This is something that God's people have believed and passed on to their children generation after generation. It's true for us, too.

Of all the Bible pictures of God watching over us, I especially like the one where Jesus prays before his betrayal and says that he is in God and God is in him and in his followers—us! So close is the watch that God keeps over us. As close as those who held me when I was sick as a child. So close is God watching.

I feel God watching now. I believe you feel it too.

Let go of the pain

I feel your pain. I do. I felt it again last night.

I dreamed I was beside someone whose whole body was suddenly tormented by great pain. I saw the pain as it crept through all of her, and I felt pain in her face and eyes, and in the way she held her body. I reached to hold her to myself, and I felt the flow of energy in her struggle, fight against her will, and lock her into a rigid posture. I held her until I could feel her pain and her cold inside myself. I felt it all. I believe the dream was about you.

I dreamed I felt your pain, and in holding you I took some pain from you. When I woke I still felt your pain in me. I want to carry that pain along with you, feel it with you, and take it from you.

Let me hold you from here, in my mind and in prayer, so you can let the pain go. In the dream I held you until you were warm, until life and health flowed through you as before, until you were at peace. Let me hold you that way in my thoughts and prayers—even from this distance. Love knows no distance. From here I can receive your pain and help you carry the hurt and fear.

There is someone else nearby who will hold you, someone who wants to feel your pain, to take your pain from you.

The New Testament Gospels contain many stories about tormented persons who let go of their pain when Jesus came near. Jesus is holding you. And I hold you in my mind and prayers.

Let go of your pain.

Fear and love

I am scared when you are scared. How do you feel when you're scared? How do you look?

I know the pain of being frightened. I know how it looks and feels to be scared. Fear shows in my eyes, in my complexion. My breathing follows my frightened feelings: it turns shallow and uneven, it loses its normal rhythm. This imbalance in oxygen spreads through my whole body. Parts of my body feel different, seem separated. I focus on them as if they are diseased and no longer part of me. I feel like I don't belong. My trust disappears, connections break, confidence weakens, love loses heart. When I'm scared I come apart.

When I'm feeling scared, I look for trust. I try to pull myself together, to become whole, to become one. I focus on belonging. God created me to belong, to be at home, to be loved. The greatest weapon against fear is love. Know that God loves you. Believe you are loved, trust it. Picture someone you trust loving you, being with you. Let their love be God's love for you. Fear is far weaker than love. Love casts out fear.

Sometimes in the night when I'm scared and the world seems like a bad dream, I light a candle or I turn on a lamp. The sight of familiar objects can help dispel nightmares and fear. In the light, a real world comes to life around me, inside me. And I remember that I am loved.

The presence of a loving face or voice helps me reconnect and belong. Speaking a prayer out loud can help me remember that God is real, that God is near. Reading an old letter from a friend or paging through family photos can remind me of their love and reassure me. How quickly fear enters our lives. How swiftly an exercise of love will cast out our fear.

Even while you read this letter, fear can leave you—can be cast out of you.

With all my heart I tell you: love casts out fear.

Take a chance

Three years ago, when the urologist said, "Herb, you have cancer," my mind spun. I had brand new thoughts. In a matter of days, I began to see things and people in a brand new way. I saw a flyer that described what I was discovering: "Being sick is a chance of a lifetime. It's a time to make your best choices."

You said you were doing things you hadn't done before. Right now you're going slower, seeing more, noticing. You're making good choices.

That's what I'm wanting for us both: good choices, the chance of a lifetime. Illness is our time to try new things, to make new discoveries, to pamper our dreams. I'm looking at an easel and paintbrush given to me for Christmas ten years ago. I'm writing country songs I've always wished to write.

This is a healing time and a discovering time. Now is a chance to be more open, to ask and to listen. Now is a time to be a friend of God: thanking, reflecting, asking, listening. I sense a spirit of gentleness in you when we talk. Gentleness is a quality. Recovery time is quality time.

I know from years of visiting in hospitals as a minister, that sick people begin to think and talk about what's important. So when they return home, they are more interested in family and friends, themselves, hope, life, love. Sick people often discover insights about spiritual topics that ministers spend years trying to learn in a seminary. This is a time to be nearer to God.

I have felt closer to my family during illness and recovery. It's a time to explore who we are as a family, to learn about love, to try going places together, having fun, learning new ways of caring. We can grow in healing times, if we use the times as a chance to discover.

Your garden is in full bloom. You've had rain and sun. Every plant is taking advantage of what it is destined to be. Flowers show us how to take a chance, to be everything possible.

Trust in God.

A blessing for you

I bless you with a Polish blessing! Here are the first lines of this old blessing-prayer:

> May the land be fertile
> Beneath your feet.
> May your days be gentle
> As the sun-kissed dew.
> May your hand be outstretched
> To all you meet.

Those words have inspired me to write a blessing for your health:

> May this night hold you softly
> As a cotton purple quilt
> And dawn wake you kindly
> With a kiss of morning sun.

Night and morning are your family. They rocked you and woke you at your birth. My blessing to you continues:

May the Spirit of God
As wind from east to west
Purify you inside out
And as water,
Bathe you from feet to face.

The spirit or breath of God is your parent. There is one
Spirit which all may breathe. God's Spirit is our life.

May you be sung to by cherubs
Who come when your heart needs a song,
And may you be attended by seraphs
Who bring foods that delight and heal.

There are always the angels, messengers of God's blessing.
Angels sing. You sing. Music has been your blessing.

Bless you.

Play in the dark

I wrote you once that night is a friend. Tonight is a friend to me. I have been remembering the dark nights when I was a child in the country. I liked our strong outdoor light, high on a pole, in the yard where we played when company came. We ran in and out of the dark for fun.

Tonight I am writing to say that we still play in the dark.

Do you remember how it felt to hide in the dark, then sneak in to "home" in a game of tag, or to get caught while running in and out of the dark? Remember?

Tonight I lay in the dark of my room. I closed my eyes to enjoy the dark. With my eyes closed I found a night sky I haven't watched for years. I took a walk in moonlight with a loved one. I have not walked under a full moon for twenty years. I watched people from my life going to work, coming home from their jobs in the night. Tonight, night is my friend.

Do you know the dark by heart? Do you know the miracles and wonders of the night sky, the ocean at night, a lake and a loon at night, flowers and birds at night?

I once had a cat that I wished would take me along on his night prowls. When I heard an owl the other night, I wanted to sit beside it and see and feel what owls know.

What does your garden do in the night? Do blossoms stay open? What happens to a leaf when dew falls gently in the dark? Have you watched the path of stars for more than an hour at night?

I am writing to you tonight. I know that you are sometimes awake, that you sometimes can't sleep. So I feel near you in the dark. If we close our eyes we can be together under the night sky.

What a miracle God gives in imagination. How good that we played in the dark, learned to love the dark, when we were little. Sometime write me a letter in the night.

In the hospital you saw how much patients can heal during one night. Yes, healing also happens in the dark.

I wish you sweet dreams.

All kinds of prayers

I'm thinking of brand new prayers. Homemade prayers. Originals. Prayers that I start which keep going, keep rambling, as if on their own. Sometimes they are full sentences; and sometimes they're phrases, words, sighs, feelings, laughter.

Do you like praying this way—rambling as though talking to yourself, even though you know it's not just yourself? I like prayers that feel like riddles, like poems, prayers that might look like posters if printed on paper. Sometimes I like prayer that doesn't worry about punctuation, sentence structure, or grammar. That's the kind of praying I'm writing about to you today.

This morning I woke at two a.m. I couldn't sleep, and then I didn't want to sleep. I prayed until three and then four. Clocks kept striking; I rambled on and on—remembering, thanking, begging, listening, planning. The prayer was full of feelings and friends. I took matters directly to God in my own words. In the middle of the second hour of praying, I slept. My happiest prayers are often born in the dark. It's an easy time to talk personally.

I had this same two a.m.-prayer-feeling when I was little, when mother and I talked on Mondays. We talked and rambled in the little washhouse while water boiled and mother's home-made lye soap perfumed the room. We talked deeply to the hum of an old washing machine with a hand ringer.

Do you sometimes ramble when praying? Do you wake in the night and pray? Can you go to sleep in the middle of praying? Please, tell me how you pray.

I am a dreamer. Pray on.

The gift of a smile

While I am healing I glance in the mirror and think about how I look. I've been noticing my smile. Do you ever wish you would smile more? I wish I would. Sometimes I am more grateful than I appear to be. Do you understand?

I've noticed that some people show their gratitude quickly. I know someone at work who has deep smiling lines. I thought they were dimples, those lines that have mapped her years of smiles. If she ever becomes angry, I believe she smiles first. I call her "Glad" for fun. Smiling has marked her face.

Sometimes I tell myself, "You are happy. Show it!" And I do. I make myself say glad words that were stuck inside.

Show your smile lines today. Mark where they are on your face. The lines on my face often show wonderment, pondering, thinking. Even when my heart is glad, my smiling lines are not always there. The woman I call "Glad" smiles by heart, and the smile marks have stayed. They came from down inside. That's where my smiles sometimes hide—down inside. Today I wish to smile inside out. As I write you, I feel my laughter lines growing inside. And now I'm smiling. Thank you.

A glad heart is a healer. God gave us the gift of smiles. Our smile is a beauty mark.

By the way, I do like your smile.

A prayer pattern

You say we're so far apart: "2000 miles." When I think about that distance and imagine driving 2000 miles, it does seem far.

Remember traveling cross-country, the telephone poles ticking time like a metronome? Distances were part of the fun of going places. I liked getting there, but I also liked the ride.

You're right. When we're healing, the distance that separates friends often seems farther.

On the other hand, we don't have to drive for days to get together. We're there. All the time it takes to get there, we can spend being there. Believe me, I am with you.

Distance and time have a magic in them. They are more fluid than water, and more pliable than plastic dough. Believe me, I am with you. You are here with me. What you want to say, I am hearing. What you want to do, I am doing with you. There is a road faster than I-94, or Interstate 80. There is a flight pattern faster than a jet stream. We have mental airways.

We have a prayer route. No roadblocks, washouts, detours, stop signs. We can meet anywhere along that route. You and I can be in five places at once, together in spirit, smiling, sharing. We can close our eyes and go back together, go ahead together, be together—even though we're 2000 miles apart.

Now that I know you, I can be with you in all the places you have told me you knew, lived, sang. I am with you. I am saying that to you today. Remember it.

And remember that someone else is with us all along the prayer route.

These are God's words, too: "I am with you."

A PRAYER PATTERN

Feeling and thinking

You ask if my mind and emotions ever touch, ignite, fire. Yes. Yes. And when they do, I say aloud how I feel about my thoughts and how I think about my feelings.

This letter is about connecting thinking with feeling.

"You have cancer," the doctor said to me. Suddenly I was flooded with feelings of fear. I was confused, dumbfounded. My mind went into neutral. My feelings broke open in chaos and painted an image in my mind like a thick, living mural. My mind became a huge oil smear, new and wet, with all the colors running and mixing. My mental canvas spun, my thoughts blurred. I grabbed onto the spinning image and held it to myself. I held myself and looked into myself: I was a mirror of the painting within.

Then someone else came near. Held me, steadied me. We looked at the cancer painting together. We were quiet. This was not about words. Colors slowed. Patterns began to form. I relaxed. I knew a peace. Life unfolded like new.

When the doctor said, "You have cancer," my soul flew like a feather in a tornado. My vision blurred. I let go. I was in a free-fall, inside an awesome euphoria. I knew: I am mortal. I felt: I am mortal. And yet I felt and knew at the same time: I am immortal. I fell inside the hand of God. I said in a whisper, "Herb has cancer." It was something I would now think about, feel, accept.

That is what I wish for you when you hear a word you wished never to hear. I wish you a free-fall—joyful, reckless, hopeful—inside God's outstretched hand. When colors burst inside you, may they be a rainbow.

I am thinking about you and feeling close.

Prescription for laughter

Thank you for reminding me of our last time together. I forgot how much we laughed until you mentioned the fun. And fun is medicine.

Today I had a checkup. My doctor and I talk when I have my checkups. Today he told me about a natural medicine deep inside the brain. Before I was born, while I was growing inside my mother, the medicine formed as enzymes in my brain. Enzymes can flood the bloodstream, flow to nerve endings, heal body cells. We hold the key to the enzyme medicine cabinet. The key is the thoughts and words we choose.

The medicine is always present. We can release it with a hearty laugh, a song, a smile, a glad thought, by whistling or humming a favorite tune. Joy sets the medicine flowing. Within seconds, healing pours through the body. Everyone has access to this personal medicine.

Do you watch the news with amazement, as I do, seeing poor and starving children smile when given the smallest morsel of food? Suddenly they are laughing and playing, their faces transformed by their joy. They giggle to get well.

So it is with you and me today. We laugh, and the medicine cabinet opens inside.

Today I prescribe for you and me: have a good laugh, do something joyful. Have fun. Hear a joke. Listen to a song. Hum. Smile. I believe I'm alive because of all the laughter enzymes so often released in me.

When I was five, I crawled out on the limb of a mulberry tree to get the ripest berries. I discovered I couldn't get down on my own. The fire department came to my rescue. The whole town came out to cheer me down. That was my first time out on a limb.

You were born with the gift of laughter. The "ha-ha" in you is older and stronger than the "oh-oh."

Have fun.

Ways to grow stronger

We talked about being strong, ways of getting back strength, feeling energy return. Here's the miracle: something unexpected happened to give me strength.

This is what I did to be strong: I opened my hands, opened my feelings, opened myself. I surrendered. I made myself vulnerable.

When I opened myself up, I received. I saw what was all around me, and I took it into myself. I felt what others were bringing me in our life together, and I loved it. I remembered gifts for which I'd not given thanks, and so I thanked. I took what I'd missed enjoying before. I cried for what I'd failed to feel. All this richness was there, and when I opened myself to it, I became stronger.

When I surrendered I became stronger. I quit spending energy on past anger, and discovered new power for living in the present. I stopped fighting weather and seasons, and suddenly nature came to me with aromas, colors and winds of beauty. I opened my hands and spread my arms to the west. Sunsets thrilled me while I stretched into the end of the day. As I stood there, I was made stronger. I tasted the psalms of God.

I became more vulnerable and was made strong. I became weak with the weary, silent with the quiet, wanting with the hungry. I cried with the sorrowing and danced with the joyful. I stayed close to those around me. Together in our weakness we became stronger. I put away my fear of weakness, and I recalled a promise I'd forgotten: "I will not test you beyond what you are able." In being vulnerable I found a strength that lifted me.

You said, "Help me be strong." I believe what I write here will help you grow strong. Much of this I learned by being with you.

As you read this, I am open to your spirit, to your prayers. I feel strong. In the receiving comes the power.

Be strong in the Lord.

Rest and sleep

Summer leaves are turning. New colors are appearing in the green woods near our home. Every tree and bush has its own new color code. Fields of foliage will soon be in October dress. Valleys and forests will be finger-painted with splashes and dabs of red and gold. Autumn is nearly here.

Autumn always arrives with color. So does spring, as the earth blooms with flowers and with green. Between these is winter. In December forests seem asleep, at rest.

Rest and sleep. That's what I'm thinking of today in writing you. We, too, cycle through the seasons. We are active; we are dormant. We sleep; we wake.

There was a time I was afraid to rest and sleep. Afraid I would not wake up. Afraid that in sleep I would lose control of my life. I talked with someone. Doctor Harold listened until he knew just what to ask. What I needed and wanted was to trust my sleep. The enemy would not let me trust. The enemy was my need to control—to manipulate—what I could not: my life. I wanted control; I needed trust.

Doctor Harold listened and asked more questions. Months passed. I learned to trust, to sleep. I learned to let go of the control. Rest returned. I love sleep, napping, rest. Controlling is tiring. Trust brings us the gift of life.

Life is not meant to be controlled. Life is a gift to be received, from a giver we can trust. As I write you, I recall a wonderful declaration of trust: "For yours is the kingdom and the power and the glory forever. Amen."

Remember the talk we once had about the word "Amen"? Amen means "truly, surely, count on it, yes." Amen means trust.

The maple in my front yard will be a yellow bouquet in two weeks. It's been that way every autumn since we planted it. I can count on the leaves turning bright yellow. Amen.

Amen to you!

Seasons for healing

To move ahead we need also to look back. I knew a gifted but illiterate woman who often advised: "You gotta look back to see where you is going." I thought of her when I heard you say, "I'm planting tulips." Perennials. Each spring they grow from the root, the bulb. They look back into their roots to see where they're growing.

You have roots: a family history, the stories of your children. Old roots live in us. We reach back to our family forebears and our spiritual ancestors for a sense of tradition, vision, energy—a sense of who we are and where we are headed.

The tulip roots here are storing for the future. Jack Frost will soon be painting window panes. Plants are bowing toward the cold. Dry stems will soon be deep in snow. The Minnesota valley near our house is growing quiet. Annuals wait in tiny seeds. Perennials wait sleeping deep inside their roots.

You are planting perennials. Bulbs. Each bulb holds generations of a plant's history. Tucked inside each bulb is beauty—a miracle—that will reappear in spring. So it is in you.

Within you is love you inherited, faith and trust that were passed on to you, habits planted early. How much good we have inside us to draw on, to tap, after a winter rest.

Forecasters predict a short winter this year. Spring will come soon; and with it, will come the sun, the green new buds, and early violets.

God gives us four seasons, a calendar for healing. Keep your eye on the tulip for good growing patterns. I think of all this when you say, "I'm planting tulips."

Tulips need their winter rest.

The smell of fresh bread

Today is Monday. Monday is the day my mother baked bread. On Mondays I can smell bread and taste the honey and see the homemade butter melting into warm slices of bread. Fresh bread was my medicine when I was little—if I ever needed medicine. And I did.

The whole world on that country hillside changed for me when my mother cut into the warm loaf. And for a while I was in heaven. Do you remember something like that from your childhood?

Aroma. What a wonderful friend, stimulant, healer. Aroma the healer, brings memories of pleasant times: blossoms, summer seasons, country gardens, kitchens, special company, bakeries down the street, a city diner, a birthday cake, a spring rain. How did all those aromas of the past stay with us? How do they manage to carry us back to places of healing?

How close we are to these healing places: the aroma of hot chocolate, of fresh apples, a vegetable bin, a Christmas tree, flickering candles, can take us there. Can you remember the smell of a forest, an old book you loved, a cold snap, autumn leaves? I can still smell the parlor in Aunt Minnie's house from fifty years ago. I loved the smell of my mother's bread back then. I loved the smell of autumn leaves when we jumped deep into them, rolled and laughed in them together. Do you remember such times?

No wonder the aroma of incense was an offering of God's people. Aromas are a blessing. I like the smell of holy communion: the bread and wine, the candles, incense, and flowers on the altar.

I know the oak tree is turning color. I wonder if it has an oak aroma.

I send you a waft of fresh bread baked today.

What's new?

What's new?

I really mean that. What's new with you? I am thinking and doing new things.

Today I made a list of five things I no longer do well, things I did well a few years ago. You know what happens as years pass or when illness sets in. I must admit, I miss doing those five things on the list. Now I'm focusing on something new.

I made a list of ten new things I want to do in the next years. The list will lengthen with time. I have the need and desire to do these new things. They are as important to me now as the five on my other list once were. Next time we talk, ask me, "What's new?"

Today I also looked back even further into my life history, to see what I enjoyed doing when I was young. It dawned on me again that we trade our past for our future. That's life.

When we talk next time, let's compare such lists. Tell me some of the things you have time to do now, things you want to do. Tell me what's new. Show me your list.

Years ago I knew a man named Walter, a salesperson. There came a time when he had to lie quietly in bed for many weeks. Members of our congregation gave him lists of names and needs to pray for. He became a power in our midst. People leaned on him for prayers of health. While Walter was lying in bed healing, his prayers helped many others become well.

Years pass, and there is always something new to do. Let's play tag—you're it!

It's getting cold. The oak leaves keep the same pattern. Each year they fall and then new ones form. New leaves grow out of the old oak limbs.

What's new with you?

WHAT'S
NEW?

Green turns to gold

It's well into autumn where I am. Green has turned to gold. Let's stand together and watch God decorate the earth on a giant easel. Colors are everywhere. God is a master painter.

When you name the flowers near your home, you describe their colors. You know the shades and hues of all their colors. When you talk this way, I can tell that your eyes are bringing health to you. You're looking at beauty, and beauty is healing. Colors are healing.

Today I am feeling that God is an artist.

God mixes and stirs all the colors and splashes them into your garden flowers and my October trees—pale and deep green leaves, soft yellows alongside sharp pink and bright red. I see the colors in the forest. You see them in your southern garden. God has an eye for beauty. So do we.

We have been given the gifts of awe, wonder, and delight. These are gifts that heal. I can see your smile when the first magnolia opens. I heal when an oak leaf grows red.

Today let's see the colors that have been given to us. They're free, no charge. And there's no closing time: night has color, too.

Some trees today are trimmed in gold leaf.

Keep looking at colors.

Letting go, hanging on

I cleaned a large part of my garage today. My son helped me to face a dumpster and to move on with my life.

Are you ever afraid of parting with something dear? Afraid to let it go? I understand, and I want to talk about letting go and hanging on.

I find it hard to let go of talents, of strengths I once had, of my health. It's hard for me to let go of past times, of reminders of the past. I need time to decide what to keep, what to let go. Today in the garage was not easy for me.

I have found ways to let possessions go so they are never completely gone. I hold onto some small pieces from the past. Today I preserved small pieces from my garage cleaning. As my children grew older, their shirts, jeans, pajamas, wore out. They became dust rags, which were finally tossed into discard piles that ended up in the garage. For me, each piece of clothing held memories: campouts, night prayers, bike rides, church, holidays. Each triggered feelings, times, smells, laughter, stories. I could not let them all go into the dumpster. I cut off a little piece of each garment. From these, we will make a quilt.

Each small piece will help me hold onto something of the whole garment. Cutting the tiny squares helped me hang onto what is best—the good times, good feelings—and let go of the rest. Good memories are saved.

I find other ways to hang onto treasures of the past. Many are saved inside lyrics and letters that I write. Keep this letter for the future. Hang onto some things in your past, things that make you feel well loved today. You can let go of the rest.

Your talents, your gifts, never really leave you. Somehow they are transformed, they stay inside you. Hang onto your great gifts—even if only tiny pieces of them.

Remember, small pieces can make a wonderful quilt.

God's gift of time

This is a time to notice the gift of time.

There was a time when I kept running out of time. There was too much to finish before "time was up."

Do you ever feel you're out of time, running late? Have you ever kept a watch on night and day, listening to time tick away on your arm? Tick-tock, tick-tock. Do you ever feel there's not enough time, or time's going too fast?

Time can become a trap—fixed and rigid, a deadly routine, a frantic race. Yesterday I stopped the clocks in our house, took off my watch, and followed time as if I were riding a river. I moved with the current. I had fun with time. I went through the day guided by an inner mission or vision, by circumstances, and by feelings. I danced with time and laughed with time. Time was like something new to me.

How can something so old as time become new? I'm writing to tell you. We can look at time in a new way—as a companion rather than a master. Yesterday I had enough time, and yet yesterday time flew. I felt a wonderful freedom.

Time is free. There's no charge for it. We have all been given the same amount per day. Today I am looking at time as something I can control. It is a friend.

Time is the lifetime God gives you and me. It's meant to be enjoyed, not feared.

I am forever your friend.

Recovery and discovery

Every time we talk you tell me about something new you've discovered. Healing is a time of discovery.

After my cancer surgery, my nurses spoke of a "recovery period." I named the time "discovery days." It took weeks of ups and downs. I remember one such week: tubes out, mowing the lawn, slowly chasing Frisbees, sawing a broken tree; then tubes back in, rest time, slow walking by a lake, feeding chunks of bread to Canadian geese.

I was recovering. But even more, I was also discovering—discovering the highs and lows of healing. Isn't it the same for you? As you recover, you discover.

I didn't only recover. I did more than get back to where I'd been before. I found a new and different direction. I discovered something utterly new in myself. I discovered humor that had been quiet for so long. I discovered a face I enjoyed in the mirror. I discovered someone I'd missed seeing. I discovered all my senses all over again.

I like myself better now. I am changing, growing. I am healthier. I feel younger.

How about you? When do you feel yourself grow? What do you enjoy seeing in the mirror?

In the recovery room I began to discover my senses. When I was little in school, we counted the senses. Are there only five? Today I feel there are more. I believe we have a sixth sense.

I am your partner in discovery.

Healing from inside

Winter is here. The birdhouse in the apple tree is empty. The wren family is grown and has flown south to where you live. The empty birdhouse does not seem lonely, but sounds cheerful as the snow begins to fall. I can still hear the chirping, the warbling, and see the wrens' busy journeys with sticks and string, insects and drink. How busy is the inside of a birdhouse.

How busy you are. I feel your mind turning—your emotions, hopes, frustrations, expectations. In all this, what I hear most is your cheerfulness. You are like a songbird. Your busy mind is healing your body.

A university professor gave children a creativity test. One assignment: draw a birdhouse. Children drew eagerly. Many soon were finished. Most drew pitched roofs, triangles and tiny holes with stick perches. The drawings looked like birdhouses.

One boy drew slowly, quietly, privately. He covered his paper all the while. A picture was unfolding. When asked how he was doing, he spoke with reverence. He could barely be heard. "I'm drawing the birdhouse from the inside." His drawing felt like what I'm hearing and feeling as I see snow fall on the birdhouse. I'm seeing the birdhouse from the inside.

When the boy finished the inside, he drew a circle around the drawing. It was the birdhouse hole. Inside was his glorious bird world.

This is a picture of our healing: we get well from inside out. From your cheerful voice I have a picture of you getting well inside out.

Reverently, me.

Music is a healer

Think of the songs you know by heart. Remember tunes you like. Music heals.

My early life in the country in Nebraska was full of music. So it seems now. I filled my days with humming and singing spirituals. On Sundays I joined full force in old hymns accompanied by a pump organ. I remember songs hummed softly when I was ill. When I helped clean the country church, I sang to the rhythm of my dusting cloth. I cleaned better when singing, and I felt better.

Do you still like to dance?

Rhythm and good lyrics and tunes heal. The biblical psalms were songs meant to heal, forgive, excite, comfort. Many of the psalms were danced, shouted, wept. I like this stanza inside Psalms 131. It's a lullaby.

I have calmed and quieted my soul,
like a weaned child with its mother;
my soul within me is like a weaned child.

I wrote a Japanese haiku, a three-line poem. Each line has
its own image, and the syllables in the three lines are five, seven,
five. It is for you.

Now absorbs all time.
Yesterday tomorrow meet.
Dance our bread and wine.

The Oak is heavy with snow. I wrote you a song. Hum
it a tune.

I am your song writer in the snow.

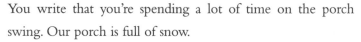

Shadows made by light

You write that you're spending a lot of time on the porch swing. Our porch is full of snow.

You like the shade on the north side of your house, the porch shade. I know the feeling of swinging through shade on a warm night. I need shade and shadows. Both have helped me through the years.

I especially like shadows in summer. I like walking beside my shadow, watching its acrobatic precision. I like its fixed stance, stubborn obedience. It moves in the sunlight. Light and shadow are a dance of two.

When I was little, my friends and I herded cows along a railroad track. We tied gunny sacks against a fence and sat under them near where the cows were grazing. We sat cool in the shade we'd made. If a tree was large enough, we sat in its shadow. We loved the comfort of shade on the hot summer days. No wonder psalm writers in ancient Israel made up songs about shade and shadows and the heat and cool of the day.

The shadows I like most come near the end of day, when the sun goes down and a breeze moves through the shadow over you. I'm glad it's comfortable where you are. Cherish any place of comfort. A swing on a porch is a healing place, especially when you're almost well.

I am writing to you at two in the morning. Here there are healing shadows on the snow beneath a full moon. Moonlight over oak trees paints shadows on snow. This is a night for reflection. There's a beauty outside tonight which most people will not see.

Sometime stand in a shadow and watch the shade from inside. Shadows are awesome, fragile, so temporary. They fade so soon. Shade is the other side of light.

Good night, again.

Hug your name

Sometimes I really feel special. It's a great feeling, so deep inside, so safe. Someone wonderful helps put it there.

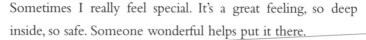

When I was little I was called Herbert. Not Herb, not Brokering. My mother stretched the word out with good feelings. I liked my name, Herbert, when she called me.

I know you also have a name you like, and you like the way it sounds when someone special says it. Listen for a good feeling when you hear someone call your name today.

My Aunt Cora helped me enjoy my name. She sewed and stuffed a white cloth puppy for me. On its tummy she stitched my name, Herbert. Think of it: my own name, hand-sewn in red! My name became my favorite word. Herbert. Herbert. She tucked the good feeling inside me in bright red thread. I hugged the puppy night after night, hugging my name and myself, my whole world. I slept hugging myself. Whenever I was ill, my puppy was there.

You know a feeling like that. Who helped you hug your name when you were little? Who made you like your name just by the way they said it? Hold onto the good sound of your name, let it make you feel good today.

I can tell you are healing. You said you're putting together a puzzle. One thousand pieces. A puzzle is a steady friend that you can always come back to. It's always waiting for you. I remember exactly where my white Herbert puppy waited in our house.

It's a winter night here. In this letter we're talking about what's warm and comforting: a puzzle, a puppy. It's a time for snuggling. You know how it felt to be close to a parent or friend or favorite blanket when getting well. So picture someone's warm word, touch, or hug, and snuggle up with it.

Have a hug.

The thank-you cure

Thanks. Before anything else, I say: Thank you. Thanks for letting me write you. Thanks for reading what I write.

During my last stay in the hospital, I noticed something about myself. Some days I was so centered on myself I forgot to say thanks. I hurt too much. I was too afraid. A friend helped me change. Whenever she visited me, she acted thankful—was thankful. She said "thank you" aloud to others, and she said it often.

In saying thanks, she gave me more than she knew. Her thankfulness was catching; I caught the cure. Giving thanks is healing. With thankfulness comes the feeling of happiness. The face feels open, relaxed. Spirits get lifted up. When we're grateful, we pray better. We remember good times, good persons, and good experiences. Thanking is good medicine. Thanks finds music, makes poems, sings. Thanks cheers, waves, dances.

That was years ago, that stay in the hospital. But I can still hear my friend's voice. She taught me a wonderful cure. Now I say thanks, and I look for thanks in others. I look for it in eyes—no words, just a quiet, joyful look. I look for it in hands—no words, just a clasp, a hug, a touch.

We give thanks, we receive thanks. Both are good. Both make well.

I'm thankful for you.

A world in bloom

Winter is leaving us at last. Days are growing longer, the sun rises earlier. Earth knows the difference. The wind is warming.

Today I let your phone ring longer than usual. I wanted to be sure you'd have time to answer. You came from the garden. You said the spring was well underway in Louisiana. You described every flower in bloom. You told of the robins gathering, as they do every winter, before they fly north. You said they were early and would come to us soon. You forecast an early springtime here. The robins and the blossoms connected us.

What you said to me through all of that was this: "I am well." Your voice was as open as the daffodils you spoke of. I could feel your face smile as you painted the azaleas. Your voice sang as you told of robins feeding to fly north. I cannot forget how well you sounded as I listened.

Then you said that work gives people worth. That is your work—the garden. Not only seeding it but seeing it. Your work and worth is touching the blossoms, smelling the peonies, making bouquets. The flowers give you worth.

No wonder flowers are the gifts brought to us when we are sick. Flowers are the seed, the sun, the earth, the rain. All these are in the bouquet. Your yellow daffodils are the clouds, the sky, the nights, the dawn, the dew. These are the work of God for us.

Your flowers are blooming. I will watch my seed up north the more. You said that the robins are feeding to fly. I will listen closely for a robin song.

I phoned to see if you are well. You have made me well.

Healing is a circle

You said you liked my letters.

"They are healing in a circle," I said. "You get love from someone, you give it back."

You said: "Or you pass it on to someone else."

Thank you. That is a greater picture of healing: we pass it on, we multiply the healing.

I began by sending you one letter each day for twelve days. And I kept writing. You have saved the letters in a file. You call them "Our Letters." "Our" is a circle word for healing. Healing is round, communal. We help others heal, and we are healed. Health swirls, spirals, cycles, loops.

Think of the magnitude of any healing: an enormous circle that spirals out from God—its fixed center—and takes in a world of light, words, medicine, images, moods, thoughts, spirit, trust. Our healing depends on what we say, know, tell, fear, believe, give, receive, touch, taste, smell, drink. Healing requires gratitude, honor, ecstasy, reverence, awe, wonder, respect, integrity, beauty, music, love, adoration.

Health is also about the circle that is us—our outside and our inside, our house and our spirit living together in peace. Healing is about past and future, history and hope, alpha and omega.

That's what these letters have been about: a circle of harmony, of balance. Healing is ultimately a good relationship in a healthy circle, with God at its center. Healing is wholeness, peace, holiness. Together we have made these letters a means of grace from God.

Thank you for being part of my healing circle.

Plant a celebration tree

What do we do to celebrate healing?

Let's plant a tree. You are coming up to visit your daughter. We'll plant a tree in some corner of her yard. A blue spruce.

Years will pass. We'll visit the tree together whenever you come north. At Christmas children will decorate the spruce with birdseed. A bird will nest there, spiders will spin webs in the branches. Your tree will grow against the sky, cast shadows onto the lake water, bear seed. Full moons and sunrises will bless the branches.

You're feeling well. Let's plant a tree and give it a name. Remember my earlier letter about our tree named Phileo?

My father planted trees wherever we lived. I watered them, watched them grow, named them. We always returned to visit them when we moved to new homes. Trees grow the same way we do: they give and take, they stretch out, look for light, drink from roots, burst into new life.

While I was healing from bypass surgery, I made a pilgrimage behind what was once the Iron Curtain. Our travel group helped plant a tree in Dresden, a city that was nearly destroyed by fire bombing in World War II. The tree was a sign of reconciliation and healing. A hole had been dug near the edge of a large open yard. The people of Dresden wanted the tree off to the side. They said: "The open space is a memorial to God." We planted the tree off to the side; we honored God.

That is why I want to plant a tree with you—as a sign of healing, a memorial to God. To thank God for you, with you. We have both been healed in these weeks and months and years. The tree will be our sign of gratitude and our reminder.

Someone will water the tree. And the blue spruce will care for them.

You take care. I'm thinking of you.

PLANT A
CELEBRATION
TREE